Cat Crazy:

Reflections on
Our Feline Friends

Edited by Heather Russell-Revesz

BARNES
& NOBLE
BOOKS
NEW YORK

The quotes in this book have been drawn from many sources, and are assumed to be accurate as quoted in their previously published forms. Although every effort has been made to verify the quotes and sources, the publisher cannot guarantee their perfect accuracy.

2003 Barnes & Noble Books

ISBN 0-7607-4729-6

Printed and bound in the United States of America

M 9 8 7 6 5 4 3 2

HAD YOU ASKED ME LAST YEAR IF I WERE A CAT person, the answer would have been no. Not that I hated cats, but I always thought of myself as a dog person without the time to have a dog.

That was B.T. (before Thelma).

My husband suggested getting a cat one day after a hard winter of dealing with mice in our 100+-year-old house. It seemed like a practical solution. Luckily, Jessi, a friend from work, fixed us up with a cat owner who wasn't able to care for her ten-year-old calico cat any longer. One fateful day in February, a tiny furry creature with green eyes and a really loud meow was handed over to us. It was Thelma.

I had absolutely no idea what I was in for. I admit to laughing at cat-owning friends who insisted their cats had individual (and interesting) personalities. *Come on, it's a cat,* I would think.

But after the initial weeks of hiding in our basement, Thelma came upstairs, and suddenly it seemed *we* were living with *her*, and not the other way around. Now I am a fully reformed cat-lover. I swear she talks to me, and even scarier, I think I understand her.

Cat Crazy was inspired by my cat. She even helped me write it (and as most cat-lovers will understand, by "helped" I mean sat on the keyboaaaerldskdjclkj;a.....).

–*Heather Russell-Revesz*

In the Beginning–
The Historical Cat

What sort of philosophers are we who know absolutely nothing of the origin and destiny of cats?

—HENRY DAVID THOREAU

The mystical character of the cat has challenged attention, delighting her admirers and terrifying her detractors, since she strolled rather suddenly and magnificently into history about 1600 B.C.

—CARL VAN VETCHEN, *The Tiger in the House*

Thou art the Great Cat,
The Avenger of the Gods,
And the Judge of Words...

—Inscription on the royal tombs of the
XIX and XX dynasties at Thebes in Egypt

In Thailand, the cat was considered the carrier of kings' souls.... When the cat finally died, it was believed she would carry the king's soul to heaven.

—Claire Horton-Bussey and David Godfrey,
Cat Owner's Survival Manual

Sphinx of my quiet hearth! who deignst to dwell
Friend of my toil, companion of mine ease,
Thine is the love of Ra and Rameses;
That men forget dost thou remember well,
Beholden still in blinking reveries,
With somber, sea-green gaze inscrutable.

—Graham Tomson, "Le Chat Noir"

The animal which the Egyptians worshipped as divine, which the Romans venerated as a symbol of liberty, which Europeans in the ignorant Middle Ages anathematized as an agent of demonology, has displayed to all ages two closely blended characteristics—courage and self-respect.

—SAKI (H. H. MUNRO), *The Square Egg*

I am the Cat which fought hard by the Acacia Tree in Heliopolis on the night when the foes of the Setting Sun were destroyed.

Who is this Cat?

This male Cat is the Sun-god Ra himself and he was called Mau because of the speech of the god Sa concerning him: He is like unto that which he hath made, therefore did the name Ra become Mau.

—*THE BOOK OF THE DEAD*, ca. 3000 B.C.

Pussy was a goddess in old Egypt,
and she has never forgotten it.
Old incense perfumes her soft fur.
A goddess in exile, she exacts honour
as any queen who has lost a realm
but will have her court and its courtiers.

—OSWALD BARRON, English writer

From history's perspective, describing Egypt as cat-friendly is like saying that Switzerland welcomes bank deposits. It was here, according to archaeologists, that cats first wandered in from the desert and deigned to become domesticated, a good four or five thousand years ago.

—CHRISTOPHER WREN,
The Cat Who Covered the World

The Cat is a victim of misunderstanding; who has never been really appreciated since Bubastis flourished; who has never taken her proper place in society...this the cat resents.

—GEORGE ROBEY, *Jokes, Jibes, and Jingles Jugged*

Cats exercise...a magic influence upon highly developed men of intellect. This is why these long-tailed Graces of the animal kingdom, these adorable, scintillating electric batteries have been the favorite animal of a Mohammed, Cardinal Richlieu, Crebillon, Rousseau, Wieland.

—LEOPOLD VON SACHER-MASOCH, *Venus in Furs*

Cat-lovers will no doubt point out that the elegance and dignity of cats are the consequence of their sojourn in the temples of the gods, where their attitudes and movements were regarded as divine prognostications.

—PHILIPPE DIOLÉ, French biologist,
"At the Service of the Heart"

The eye of a cat is an eye in the forest and in all time, and so even the stupidest cat seems to know more than any dog or horse; it knows history.

—ELEANOR CLARK, "Piazza Vittorio"

A Cat's Nature

i have got you out here
in the great open spaces
where cats are cats.

—Don Marquis, "mehitabel has an adventure"

It is in the nature of cats to do a certain amount
of unescorted roaming.

—Adlai Stevenson

A widow kept a favourite cat.
 At first a gentle creature;
But when he was grown sleek and fat,
With many a mouse, and many a rat,
 He soon disclosed his nature.

—JONATHAN SWIFT,
"The Fable of the Widow and Her Cat"

Cats are the ultimate narcissists.

—JAMES GORMAN,
"The Sociobiology of Humor in Cats and Dogs"

"Ah! I see everybody likes what he was bred to," sighed the Cat. "I was bred to do nothing, and I must like that."

—JAMES ANTHONY FROUDE, *The Cat's Pilgrimage*

[A cat is] the emblem of restlessness and impatience at the same moment.

—ALEXANDRE DUMAS, *The Three Musketeers*

Animals are ever so psychic.... The cats particularly. They seem to know. You can fool everybody, but...you can't fool a cat. They seem to know who's not right, if you know what I mean.

—PET STORE OWNER, *Cat People* (1943),
Dewitt Bodeen and Jacques Tourneur

A happy arrangement: many people prefer cats to other people, and many cats prefer people to other cats.

—MASON COOLEY, aphorist, *City Aphorisms*

Nature breaks through the eyes of the cat.

—IRISH PROVERB

Beware in the presence of cats: they never give, they do not even retaliate—they only reply, and purr in doing so.

—FRIEDRICH NIETZSCHE

Cattributes

A cat has absolute honesty.

—ERNEST HEMINGWAY

Cats seem to go on the principle that it never does any harm to ask for what you want.

—JOSEPH WOOD KRUTCH, *Twelve Seasons*

The Cat was a creature of absolute convictions, and his faith in his deductions never wavered.

—MARY E. WILKINS FREEMAN, "The Cat"

It is easy to understand why the rabble dislike cats. A cat is beautiful; it suggests ideas of luxury, cleanliness, voluptuous pleasures...

—CHARLES BAUDELAIRE, *Intimate Journals*

If a fish is the movement of water embodied, given shape, then a cat is a diagram and pattern of subtle air.

—DORIS LESSING, *Particularly Cats*

If your cat's tail is swishing rapidly from side to side, it signifies: impatience, fury, serious playfulness (mock stalking), or, in some cases, DefCon5.

—STEPHEN J. SPIGNESI, *The Cat Book of Lists*

The cat is cryptic and close to strange things which men cannot see.

—H. P. LOVECRAFT

Nothing is more determined than a cat on a hot tin roof.

—Tennessee Williams

For all cats have this particularity, each and every one, from the meanest ally sneaker to the proudest, whitest she that ever graced a pontiff's pillow—we have our smiles, as it were, painted on. Those small, cool, quiet Mona Lisa smiles that smile we must, no matter whether it's been fun or it's been not. So all cats have a politician's air; we smile and smile, and so they think we're villains.

—Angela Carter, "Puss-in-Boots"

I'm sitting here like Sis cat, washing my face and usin' my manners.

—Zora Neale Hurston, *Mules and Men*

By casting in his lot with theirs he was paying them the highest compliment of which a cat is capable. It would have been the height of impoliteness not to recognize his distinguished appreciation.

–JOHN COLEMAN ADAMS, "Midshipman, the Cat"

Cats, no less liquid than their shadows
Offer no angles to the wind

–A. S. J. TESSIMOND, *Cats*

Kittens

The trouble with a kitten is
THAT
Eventually it becomes a
CAT

—Ogden Nash, "The Kitten"

In the editorial office everybody now has got a kitten from me; very well, I shall have to get taken on at another place. I am ready to put my name down for any society or organization, if they will assure me of the disposal of at least twenty-one kittens.

—Karel Čapek, "The Immortal Cat"

I don't so much mind hearing an old cat swear, but I can't bear to see a mere kitten give way to it. It seems sad in one so young.

—JEROME K. JEROME, "On Cats and Dogs"

"One, two, three," Vanya counts.
"Three kittens. So there is one for you, one for me, and one for somebody else, too."

—ANTON CHEKHOV, "An Incident"

archy she said to me
yesterday
the life of a female
artist is continually
hampered what in hell
have i done to deserve
all these kittens

—DON MARQUIS, "mehitabel and her kittens"

In the image of the lion
Made he kittens small and curious.

—HEINRICH HEINE, *Songs of Creation*

A kitten is so flexible that she is almost double;
the hind parts are equivalent to another kitten
with which the fore part plays.

—HENRY DAVID THOREAU, *Journal*

And so, poor kit!, must thou endure,
When thou becom'st a cat demure,
Full many a cuff and angry word,
Chased roughly from the tempting board.

—JOANNA BAILLIE, "The Kitten"

But the kitten, how she starts—
Crouches, stretches, paws, and darts.

—WILLIAM WORDSWORTH,
"The Kitten and the Falling Leaves"

Our old cat has kittens three—
What do you think their names should be?
Pepperpot, Sootikin, Scratchaway-there,
Was there ever a kitten with these to compare?

—THOMAS HOOD, "Choosing Their Names"

A kitten is a thing apart; and many people who lack the discriminating enthusiasm for cats, who regard these beautiful beasts with aversion and mistrust, are won over easily, and cajoled out of their prejudices, by the deceitful wiles of kittenhood.

—AGNES REPPLIER, "A Kitten"

It is a very inconvenient habit of kittens (Alice had once made the remark) that whatever you say to them, they always purr.

—LEWIS CARROLL, Through the Looking Glass
and What Alice Found There

Curiosity

Yes the Rum Tum Tugger is a Curious Cat—
And there isn't any call for me to shout it:
For he will do
As he do do
And there's no doing anything about it!

> —T. S. (THOMAS STEARNS) ELIOT,
> "The Rum Tum Tugger"

Cats are inquisitive, but hate to admit it.

> —MASON COOLEY, aphorist

Dawn follows Dawn and Nights grow old and all
the while this curious cat
Lies crouching on the Chinese mat with eyes of
satin rimmed with gold.

—OSCAR WILDE, "The Sphinx"

Curiosity killed the cat. Satisfaction brought it back.

—ENGLISH PROVERB

Curiosity killed the cat, but for a while I was a
suspect.

—STEVEN WRIGHT

Feline
Fascination

I will admit to feeling exceedingly proud when any cat has singled me out for notice; for, or course, every cat is really the most beautiful woman in the room. That is part of their deadly fascination.

—E. V. Lucas, *365 Days and One More*

The great charm of cats is their rampant egotism, their devil-may-care attitude toward responsibility, their disinclination to earn an honest dollar.

—Robertson Davies,
The Table Talk of Samuel Marchbanks

I think it well to remember that, when writing for the newspapers, we are writing for an elderly lady in Hastings who has two cats of which she is passionately fond. Unless our stuff can successfully compete for her interest with those cats, it is no good.

—WILLMOTT LEWIS quoted in
In Time of Trouble, written by Claud Cockburn

A cat cares for you only as a source of food, security, and a place in the sun. Her high self-sufficiency is her charm.

—CHARLES HORTON COOLEY, *Life and the Student*

Beautiful present sufficingness of a cat's imagination!

—LEIGH HUNT

For there is not a man living who knows better than I that the four charms of a cat lie in its closed eyes, its long and lovely hair, its silence, and even its affected love.

—HILAIRE BELLOC

I don't want her to have a cat because she'll end up talking baby talk to the cat. That's the way it is, and how can a P.I. do that?

—SUE GRAFTON, on her character Kinsey Millhone, as quoted in the *New York Times*, August 4, 1994

I saw the most beautiful cat today. It was sitting by the side of the road, its two front feet neatly and graciously together. Then it gravely swished around its tail to completely and snugly encircle itself. It was so fit and beautifully neat, that gesture, and so self-satisfied—so complacent.

—ANNE MORROW LINDBERGH, *Bring Me a Unicorn*

Whether they be musician cats in my band or the real cats of the world, they all got style.

—RAY CHARLES

An Independent Spirit

I value in the cat the independent and almost ungrateful spirit which prevents her from attaching herself to anyone...

—Vicomte de Chateaubriand

Of all God's creatures there is only one that cannot be made the slave of the lash. That one is the cat. If man could be crossed with a cat it would improve man, but it would deteriorate the cat.

—Mark Twain, *Notebook*

The Cat. He walked by himself, and all places were alike to him.

> —Rudyard Kipling,
> "The Cat That Walked by Himself," *Just So Stories*

I'd die in your warm softness. Your life of abundance is fine for spoiled cats. Free cats will never buy your ease and your comfort for the price of being imprisoned.

> —Émile Zola, "Cat's Paradise"

The cat is domestic in as far as suits its own ends; it will not be kenneled or harnessed nor suffer any dictation as to its goings out or comings in.

> —Saki (H. H. Munro), *The Square Egg*

The cat owes man nothing.

> —Paul Corey, "Cat-Watching in the Cybernetic Age"

If you are worthy of its affection, a cat will be your friend but never your slave.

—THÉOPHILE GAUTIER

The cat lives alone, has no need of society, obeys only when she pleases, pretends to sleep that she may see the more clearly, and scratches everything on which she can lay her paw.

—VICOMTE DE CHATEAUBRIAND

I'm like Cat here. We're a couple of no-name slobs. We belong to nobody and nobody belongs to us. We don't even belong to each other.

—HOLLY GOLIGHTLY (Audrey Hepburn),
Breakfast at Tiffany's, screenplay by George Axelrod

Owning a cat, especially from kittenhood, is a lot like having a child. You feed him, do your best to educate him, talk to him as if he understands you—and, in exchange, you want him to love you. He can drive you mad with his independence.

—PETER GETHERS, *The Cat Who Went to Paris*

Cattitudes

No favor can win gratitude from a cat.

—JEAN DE LA FONTAINE

Humans are fools. When I purr—now wait, this is the expression humans use. I prefer to say that they are being purred at. In any case, humans are such fools that when they are purred at by me, they mistakenly think that I love them dearly, and they do whatever I want them to. At times, they stroke my head.

—NATSUME SOSEKI, *I Am a Cat*

No man has ever dared to manifest his boredom so insolently as does a Siamese tomcat, when he yawns in the face of his amorously importunate wife. No man has ever dared to proclaim his illicit amours so frankly as this same tom caterwauling on the tiles.

—ALDOUS HUXLEY, *Collected Essays*

The vanity of man revolts from the serene indifference of the cat.

—AGNES REPPLIER, *Americans and Others*

Conscience obliges me to state that the aversion of Cats to wetting their fur was the only reason for my fashion of drinking, but we will always be badly understood by the savants who are much more preoccupied in showing their own wit, than in discovering ours.

—HONORÉ DE BALZAC,
"The Afflictions of an English Cat"

To gain the friendship of a cat is not an easy thing.

—Théophile Gautier, "A Cat's Friendship"

Cats are autocrats of naked self-interest. They are both amoral and immoral, consciously breaking rules. Their "evil" look at such times is no human projection: the cat may be the only animal who savors the perverse or reflects upon it.

—Camille Paglia, *Sexual Personae*

Ming liked best lying in the sun with his mistress on one of the long canvas chairs on their terrace home. What Ming did not like were the people she sometimes invited to their house...Ming detested people. In all the world, he liked only Elaine.

—Patricia Highsmith, "Ming's Biggest Prey"

You say chocolate
Is bad for cats, but I think
You are just greedy.

—DEBORAH COATES, *Cat Haiku*

I've never understood why women love cats. Cats are independent, they don't listen, they don't come in when you call, they like to stay out all night, and when they're home they like to be left alone and sleep. In other words, every quality that women hate in men they love in cats.

—JAY LENO

Are cats lazy? Well, more power to them if they are. Which one of us has not entertained the dream of doing just as he likes, when and how he likes, and as much as he likes?

—FERNAND MÉRY, *Her Majesty the Cat*

The Age-Old Question—
Cats or Dogs?

If animals could speak the dog would be a blundering outspoken fellow, but the cat would have the rare grace of never saying a word too much.

—MARK TWAIN

Most dogs worship their master because it's the right thing to do. A cat, by contrast, will choose to be your devoted friend.

—KAREN ANDERSON, writer

If a dog jumps up into your lap, it is because he is fond of you; but if a cat does the same thing, it is because your lap is warmer.

—ALFRED NORTH WHITEHEAD,
Dialogues of Alfred North Whitehead

Cats are admirable company. I am very fond of dogs, too; but their sphere is in the field. In the house they do not understand that repose of manner which is the soul of breeding. The cat's manners, or rather manner, seems to have been perfected by generations, nay centuries, of familiar intercourse with the great and cultivated of the earth.

—ALGERNON S. LOGAN, *Vistas from the Stream*

Now a cat will not take an excursion merely because a man wants a walking companion. Walking is a human habit into which dogs readily fall but it is a distasteful form of exercise to a cat unless he has a purpose in view.

—CARL VAN VECHTEN

When he heard people with no knowledge of the cat's character saying that cats were not a loving as dogs, that they were cold and selfish, he always thought to himself how impossible it was to understand the charm and lovableness of a cat if one had not, like him, spent many years living alone with one.

—JUN'ICHIRO TANIZAKI,
"A Cat, a Man, and Two Women"

You call to a dog and a dog will break its neck to get to you. Dogs just want to please. Call to a cat and its attitude is, "What's in it for me?"

—LEWIS GRIZZARD, "Pet Peeves"

Dogs may fawn on all and some,
     As they come;
You, a friend of loftier mind,
     Answer friends alone in kind.

—ALGERNON CHARLES SWINBURNE, "To a Cat"

Dogs often remind us of the human, all-too-human. Cats, never.

—MASON COOLEY, aphorist, *City Aphorisms*

The cat assumed a kind of ascendancy among the quadrupeds; sitting in state in Scott's armchair, and occasionally stationing himself on a chair beside the door as if to review his subjects as they passed, giving each dog a cuff beside the ears as he went by.

—WASHINGTON IRVING, "Abbotsford"

The cat is an anarchist, while the dog is a socialist. He is an aristocratic, tyrannical anarchist at that.

—CARL VAN VETCHEN

It will gratify you to know that a favourite cat keeps [the bloodhound] in the greatest possible order, insists upon all rights of precedence, and scratches with impunity the nose of an animal who would make no bones of a wolf...

—SIR WALTER SCOTT, from a letter to Joanna Baillie

The housedog he flees after me—why was I born a cat?

—C. S. Calverley

People who wish to salute the free and independent side of their evolutionary character acquire cats. People who wish to pay homage to their servile and salivating roots own dogs.

—Anna Quindlen, *Thinking Out Loud*

Weighing in on Cats—
The Lovers

In the matter of animals I love only cats, but I love them unreasonably, for their qualities and in spite of their numerous faults.

> —J. K. HUYSMANS, French novelist

There are two means of refuge from the miseries of life: music and cats.

> —ALBERT SCHWEITZER

And one thing I know is that, when Polar Bear and I do meet again, the first thing I will say to him is that he is the best cat ever. And another thing I know is that, wherever we are, he will be the best cat there, too.

—CLEVELAND AMORY, *The Best Cat Ever*

It has been proposed by a good many perceptive people that she is probably the most beautiful cat in the Western Hemisphere…and her purr, to those attuned, is the music of the spheres.

—JEAN STAFFORD, "George Eliot: A Medical Study"

Diana gives a terrible account of your cat, such a wrecker? Alas, old animals are so much nicer. I love my cat now, but it took about eight years.

—NANCY MITFORD, letter to Lady Redesdale, 1959

Every life has a love story, even though the beloved may be imaginary, or a cat.

—MASON COOLEY, aphorist

I shall never forget the indulgence with which Dr. Johnson treated Hodge, his cat, for whom he himself used to go out and buy oysters, lest the servants, having that trouble, should take a dislike to the poor creature.

—JAMES BOSWELL

I believe cats to be spirits come to earth. A cat, I am sure, could walk on a cloud without coming through.

—JULES VERNE

Ginger was as much the object of my idolatry as if she had had a temple and I had been a worshipper in ancient Egypt, but, like other deities, she was reprobated by those who were not of my faith.

—LADY SYDNEY MORGAN, *Lady Morgan's Memoirs*

Ever since she could remember, there had been Moodie, and Moodie had been hers—to be slept on, talked to, hauled about, wheeled in a doll's perambulator, read aloud to, confided in, wept on, trodden on, loved, and taken for granted.

– SYLVIA TOWNSEND WARNER, "Total Loss"

I said something which gave you to think I hated cats. But gad, sir, I am one of the most fanatical cat-lovers in the business. If you hate them, I may learn to hate you. If your allergies hate them, I will tolerate the situation to the best of my ability.

—RAYMOND CHANDLER, letter to publisher Hamish Hamilton, January 26, 1950

If I die before my cat, I want a little of my ashes put in his food so I can live inside him.

—Drew Barrymore

Both ardent lovers and austere scholars, when once they come to the years of discretion, love cats, so strong and gentle, the pride of the household, who like them are sensitive to the cold, and sedentary.

—Charles Baudelaire

"I meant," said Ipslore bitterly, "what is there in this world that truly makes living worthwhile?"

Death thought about it.

"Cats," he said eventually. "Cats are nice."

—Terry Pratchett, *Sourcery*

Momma loves morals and Papa loves cats.

—SUSY CLEMENS, daughter of Mark Twain

Weighing in on Cats—
The Others

People with insufficient personalities are fond of cats. These people adore being ignored.

—HENRY MORGAN,
quoted in *The Cat-Hater's Handbook*

Cats are intended to teach us that not everything in nature has a function.

—GARRISON KEILLOR

God save all here, barrin' the cat.

—IRISH SALUTATION

You're a very nosy fellow, kitty-cat, huh? You know what happens to nosy fellows? Huh? No? Wanna guess? Huh? No? Okay. They lose their noses.

—THE THUG IN THE WHITE SUIT (Roman Polanski), *Chinatown*

The dog is mentioned in the Bible eighteen times—the cat not even once.

—W. E. FARBSTEIN, quoted in "Hundkeit"

I'm one of those wretched people who can't stand cats. I don't mean just that I prefer dogs. I mean the presence of a cat in the same room with me makes me feel like nothing on earth.

—DOROTHY L. SAYERS, "The Cyprian Cat"

What do I care about the purring of one who cannot love, like the cat?

–Attributed to FRIEDRICH NIETZSCHE

Vengeance I ask and cry
By way of exclamation.
On all the whole nation
Of cattes wild and tame:
God send them sorrow and shame!

–JOHN SKELTON, "Philip Sparrow"

What I've got against cats…is their unreliability. They lack candor and are not square shooters. You get your cat and you call him Thomas or George, as the case may be. So far, so good. Then one morning you wake up and find six kittens in the hat-box and you have to reopen the whole matter, approaching it from an entirely different angle.

–P. G. WODEHOUSE, "The Story of Webster"

Shall I choke you, Cat,
Or kiss you?
Really I do not know.

—AMY LOWELL, "To Winky"

Pusse, I will curse thee; may'st thou dwell
With some dry Hermit in a cell.

—THOMAS MASTER, "On Lute Strings Catt-Eaten"

Unusual for him to be so effusive, but when he
did decide on it, it was always with someone who
couldn't stand cats. You'll have noticed it's a way
they have.

—ELLIS PETERS, *The Trinity Cat*

Any conditioned cat-hater can be won over by any
cat who chooses to make the effort.

—PAUL COREY, *Do Cats Think?*

Proverbs and Superstitions

A cat may looke on a King.

—ENGLISH PROVERB

"A cat may look at a king," said Alice. "I've read that in some book, but I don't remember where."

—LEWIS CARROLL, Alice's Adventures in Wonderland

A cat that catches mice does not meow.

—CHINESE PROVERB

The borrowed cat catches no mice.

—JAPANESE PROVERB

It is better to feed one cat than many mice.

—NORWEGIAN PROVERB

When a cat cries over a rat, it's a case of false compassion.

—CHINESE PROVERB

When the cat's away, the rats dance on the table.

—SWEDISH PROVERB

After eating hundreds of rats, the cat is on a pilgrimage.

—PUNJABI PROVERB

A mouse does not run into the mouth of a sleeping cat.

—ESTONIAN PROVERB

If cats had wings there would be no ducks in the lake.

—INDIAN PROVERB

Cat lufat visch, ac he nele his feth wete.
[The cat would eate fish, and would not wet her feete.]

—ENGLISH PROVERB

The cat always leaves a mark on his friend.

—AESOP

The greedy cat makes the servant girl watchful.

—FRENCH PROVERB

An overdressed woman is like a cat dressed in saffron.

—EGYPTIAN PROVERB

In speaking of his intelligence, my wife, who at heart was not a little tinctured with superstition, made frequent allusions to the ancient popular notion, which regarded all black cats as witches in disguise.

—EDGAR ALLAN POE, "The Black Cat"

Called a "familiar," from the mediæval superstition that Satan's favourite form was a black cat. Hence "witches" were said to have a cat as their familiar.

—E. COBHAM BREWER, *Dictionary of Phrase and Fable*

A Cat has nine Lives.

—Thomas Fuller, *Proverbes*

...like the cat I have nine times to die.

—Sylvia Plath, "Lady Lazarus"

The black cat does not die. Those same books, if I am not mistaken, teach that the black cat is deathless. Deathless as evil. It is the origin of the common superstition of the cat with nine lives.

—Hjalmar Poelzig (Boris Karloff), in the film *The Black Cat*

"Cats have nine lives, you know," said Sir Wilfrid heartily.

"Possibly," answered Tobermory, "but only one liver."

—Saki (H. H. Munro), "Tobermory"

At Home

A home without a cat—and a well fed, well petted and properly revered cat—may be a home, perhaps, but how can it prove title?

—MARK TWAIN

Happy is the home with at least one cat.

—ITALIAN PROVERB

There is no need for a piece of sculpture in a home that has a cat.

—WILLIAM BATES, writer

When the tea is brought at five o'clock
And all the neat curtains are drawn with care
The little black cat with bright green eyes
Is suddenly purring there.

> —Harold Munro, "Milk for the Cat"

Passion for place—there is no greater urge in feline nature.

> —Paul Annixter

Sitting drowsy in the fire-light,
winked and purred the mottled cat.

> —John Greenleaf Whittier

People are forbidden from entering a darkened house which does not have a cat living in it.

> —Talmud

A cat improves the garden wall in sunshine, and the hearth in foul weather.

—JUDITH MERKLE RILEY

Books and cats and fair-haired little girls make the best furnishing for a room.

—FRENCH PROVERB

I love cats because I enjoy my home; and little by little, they become its visible soul.

—JEAN COCTEAU

Just Who Owns Whom?

As every cat owner knows, nobody owns a cat.

—ELLEN PERRY BERKELEY, writer

A cat must be allowed and encouraged to be a cat, and everyone's going to be happier.

—KAREN ANDERSON,
Cats Have No Masters...Just Friends

Cats do, however, like routine—in fact, they love it. And, in the days—and nights—which followed the rescue, my cat and I worked out many routines. Or rather he worked them out; and I, dutifully as I could, worked at following them.

—CLEVELAND AMORY,
The Cat Who Came for Christmas

The cat who doesn't act finicky soon loses control of his owner.

—MORRIS THE CAT, 9Lives spokescat

At dinnertime he would sit in a corner, concentrating, and suddenly they would say, "Time to feed the cat," as if it were their own idea.

—LILIAN JACKSON BRAUN

He liked companionship, but he wouldn't be petted, or fussed over, or sit in anyone's lap a moment; he always extricated himself from such familiarity with dignity and with no show of temper. If there was any petting to be done, however, he chose to do it.

—CHARLES DUDLEY WARNER,
"Calvin: A Study of Character"

Life with a cat is in certain ways a one-sided proposition.... If you're not willing to humor them, you might as well stick to dogs.

—TERRY TEACHOUT, "What's New Pussycat"

The golden rule of cats that governs all relationships we have with people: you scratch my back, you scratch my back.

—DAVID FISHER, *Conversations with My Cat*

This will be an incoherent letter because I have just been given a very engaging Persian kitten, named after St. Philip Neri (who was very sound on cats) and his opinion is that I have been given to him.

—EVELYN UNDERHILL, *The Letters of Evelyn Underhill*

He is able to take thought for other cats and for his human companion—master hardly seems the right word in the case of such an animal—who is doubtless to him only a very big cat that walks erect on his hind-legs.

—W. H. HUDSON, *A Shepherd's Life*

When I play with my cat, who knows but that she regards me more as a plaything than I do her?

—MICHEL DE MONTAIGNE,
Apology for Raimond Sebond

The Hunter in the House

We tie bright ribbons around their necks, and occasionally little tinkling bells, and we affect to think that they are as sweet and vapid as the coy name "kitty" by which we call them would imply. It is a curious illusion. For, purring beside our fireplaces and pattering along our back fences, we have got a wild beast as uncowed and uncorrupted as any under heaven.

—ALAN DEVOE, in *Plain and Fancy Cats*

The most domestic cat, which has lain on a rug all her days, appears quite at home in the woods, and, by her sly and stealthy behavior, proves herself more native there than the regular inhabitants.

—Henry David Thoreau, *Walden*

The really great thing about cats is their endless variety. One can pick a cat to fit almost any kind of décor, color scheme, income, personality, mood. But under the fur, whatever color it may be, there still lies, essentially unchanged, one of the world's free souls.

—Eric Gurney, writer

But the cat is grown small and thin with desire, Transformed to a creeping lust for milk.

—Harold Munro, "Milk for the Cat"

She sights a Bird—she chuckles—
She flattens—then she crawls—
She runs without the look of feet—
Her eyes increase to Balls—

—EMILY DICKINSON

Cat! who hast pass'd thy grand climacteric,
    How many mice and rats hast in thy days
Destroy'd?—How many tidbits stolen?...

—JOHN KEATS, "On Mrs. Reynolds' Cat"

For if he meets another cat he will kiss her
    in kindness.
For when he takes his prey he plays with it to
    give it chance.

—CHRISTOPHER SMART, *Jubilate Agno*

The phrase "domestic cat" is an oxymoron.

—GEORGE WILL

She will dream of the cats' world; of the hosts of cats; of cats, when there will be enough of them, seizing power to rule the universe.

—KAREL ČAPEK, "The Immortal Cat"

Lat take a cat, and fostre hym wel with milk
And tendre flessh, and make his couche of silk,
And lat hym seen a mous go by the wal,
Anon he weyveth milk, and flesh, and al,
And every deyntee that is in that haus,
Swich appetit hath he to ete a mous.

—GEOFFREY CHAUCER, *The Canterbury Tales*

Your master grieved as though you'd
    savaged him,
When you devoured his partridge,
    wicked cat.

—DAMOCHARIS THE GRAMMARIAN
(ca. A.D. 550), *Anthologia Palatina*

He seems the incarnation of everything soft and silky and velvety, without a sharp edge in his composition, a dreamer whose philosophy is sleep and let sleep; and then, as evening draws on, he goes out into the garden with a red glint in his eyes and slays a drowsy sparrow.

—Saki (H. H. Munro),
"The Philanthropist and the Happy Cat"

A cat's rage is beautiful, burning with pure cat flame, all its hair standing up and crackling blue sparks, eyes blazing and sputtering.

—William S. Burroughs

Once upon a time there were three little singing birds in a house, but all three were devoured by the cat. It was not an ordinary cat, but a really, really devout cat.

—I. L. Peretz, *The Devout Cat*

Only skin deep lies the feral nature of the cat, unchanged still.

—HENRY DAVID THOREAU, *Journal*

But the native wildness and suspicion in him could never be wholly overcome; it continued to show itself on occasions even after I had known him for months and had won his confidence, and when it seemed that, in his wild-cat, conditional way, he had accepted my friendship.

—W. H. HUDSON, *Gip*

I sleep with two cats, and the touch of their fur brushing against my naked skin is among the most beautiful sensations I can think of. They calm me, these animals who could be wild but choose not to be, who go outside to kill and lounge around, then come home every day for the food I provide and for my touch.

—ALISON HAWTHORNE DEMING, "Exiled in America"

The Artistic Cat

Nothing is so difficult as to paint the cat's face, which as Moncrif justly observes, bears a character of "finesse and hilarity." The lines are so delicate, the eyes so strange, the movements subject to such sudden impulses, that one should be feline oneself to portray such a subject.

—CHAMPFLEURY (Jules Husson)

Balanchine has trained his cat to perform brilliant *jetés* and *tours en l'air*; he says that at last he has a body worth choreographing for.

—BERNARD TAPER, *Balanchine*

To respect the cat is the beginning of the aesthetic sense.

—Erasmus Darwin

The smallest feline is a masterpiece.

—Leonardo da Vinci

I want to create a cat like the real cats I see crossing the street, not like those you see in houses. They have nothing in common. The cat of the street has bristling fur. It runs like a fiend, and if it looks at you, you think it is going to jump in your face.

—Pablo Picasso

Because of our willingness to accept cats as superhuman creatures, they are the ideal animals with which to work creatively.

—Roni Schotter, writer and illustrator

The Bard on Cats

Let Hercules himself do what he may,
The cat will mew and dog will have his day.

—*HAMLET*, act 5, scene 1

They'll take suggestion as a cat laps milk;
They'll tell the clock to any business that
We say befits the hour.

—*THE TEMPEST*, act 2, scene 1

I am as vigilant as a cat to steal cream.

—*Henry IV, Part 1*, act 4, scene 2

A harmless necessary cat.

—*The Merchant of Venice*, act 4, scene 1

Letting I dare not wait upon I would,
Like the poor cat i' the adage.

—*Macbeth*, act 1, scene 7

Hang me in a bottle like a cat.

—*Much Ado about Nothing*, act 1, scene 1

What, courage, man! What though care killed a cat, thou hast mettle enough in thee to kill care.

—*Much Ado about Nothing*, act 5, scene 1

Some men there are love not a gaping pig,
Some that are mad if they behold a cat...

—*THE MERCHANT OF VENICE*, act 4, scene 1

Is man no more than this? Consider him well.
Thou ow'st the worm no silk, the beast no hide,
the sheep no wool, the cat no perfume.

—*KING LEAR*, act 3, scene 4

I had rather be a kitten and cry mew
Than one of these same metre ballad-mongers.

—*KING HENRY IV, PART I*, act 3, scene 1

My sister crying, our maid howling, our cat wring-
ing her hands.

—*THE TWO GENTLEMEN OF VERONA*, act 2, scene 3

The cat, with eyes of burning coal,
Now Couches 'fore the mouse's hole.

   —*PERICLES, PRINCE OF TYRE*, act 3, scene 1

I could endure anything before but a cat, and now he's a cat to me.

   —*ALL'S WELL THAT ENDS WELL*, act 4, scene 3

Poets in Praise
of Pussycats

Pussycat, pussycat, where have you been?
I've been to London to look at the Queen.
Pussycat, pussycat, what did you there?
I frightened a little mouse under the chair.

—MOTHER GOOSE,
"Pussycat, Pussycat, Where Have You Been?"

They take, brooding, the noble attitudes
Of sphinxes stretched in deepest solitudes
That look to slumber in an endless dream.

—CHARLES BAUDELAIRE, "Cats"

Bathsheba! to whom none ever said scat—
No worthier cat
Ever sat on a mat,
Or caught a rat.
Requiescat!

> —JOHN GREENLEAF WHITTIER,
> "For a Little Girl Mourning Her Favorite Cat"

The Owl and the Pussycat went to sea
In a beautiful pea-green boat,
They took some honey, and plenty of money,
Wrapped up in a five-pound note.

> —EDWARD LEAR, "The Owl and the Pussycat"

Cruel, but composed and bland,
    Dumb, inscrutable and grand,
So Tiberius might have sat
    Had Tiberius been a cat.

> —MATTHEW ARNOLD, "Atossa"

Smelly cat
Smelly cat
What are they feeding you?
Smelly cat
Smelly cat
It's not your fault…

—PHOEBE, singing the "Smelly Cat" song,
from *Friends*

flex and reflex of claws
gently pricking through sweater to skin
gently sustains their own tune,
not mine. I-Thou, cat, I-Thou.

—DENISE LEVERTOV, "The Cat as Cat"

Minnaloushe creeps through the grass
Alone, important and wise,
And lifts to the changing moon
His changing eyes.

—WILLIAM BUTLER YEATS, "The Cat and the Moon"

I had a cat named Snowball, she died, she died,
Mom said she was sleeping, she lied, she lied!
Why, oh why, is my cat dead,
Couldn't that Chrysler hit me instead?

> —LISA SIMPSON, poem for her cat Snowball,
> from *The Simpsons*

Cat stands at the fridge,
Cries loudly for milk.
But I've filled her bowl.
Wild cat, I say, Sister,
Look, you have milk.

> —FRANCES MAYES, "Sister Cat"

This set of verses, Puss, to you
I dedicate—and ask in quittance
One thing alone—'tis nothing new—
A set of quarter-Persian kittens.

> —F. C. W. HILEY, "To a Persian Cat"

What's new pussycat ? Woah, Woah

What's new pussycat ? Woah, Woah…

Pussycat, Pussycat

I love you

Yes, I do!

You and your pussycat nose!

—TOM JONES,
"What's New Pussycat," Burt Bacharach Hal David

I and Pangur Bán, my cat,
'Tis a like task we are at;
Hunting mice is his delight,
Hunting words I sit all night.

—ANONYMOUS, "Pangur Bán," ca. ninth century A.D.

To err is human, to purr feline.

—ROBERT BYRNE

The Literary Cat

The affinity of writers for cats is something that has never been satisfactorily explained.

—WILLIAM H. A. CARR

As an inspiration to the author, I do not think the cat can be overestimated. He suggests so much grace, power, beauty, motion, mysticism. I do not wonder that many writers love cats; I am only surprised that all do not.

—CARL VAN VECHTEN

They say the test of literary power is whether a man can write an inscription. I say, "Can he name a kitten?"

—SAMUEL BUTLER

Sometimes he tried to take part in the work, and would attempt to pull the pen out of my hand, no doubt in order to write himself, for he was an aesthetic cat, like Hoffman's Murr, and I strongly suspect him of having scribbled his memoirs at night on some house-top by the light of his phosphorescent eyes. Unfortunately these lubrications have been lost.

—THÉOPHILE GAUTIER,
"The Black and White Dynasties"

Let a man get up and say, "Behold, this is the truth," and instantly I perceive a sandy cat filching a piece of fish in the background. Look, you have forgotten the cat, I say.

—VIRGINIA WOOLF, *The Waves*

If I were cat, thou human creature—
I should, like thee, be no great mouser,
And thou, like me, no great composer.

—HARTLEY COLERIDGE, "To a Cat"

One of these kittens was kept, who, as he was quite deaf, was left unnamed, and became known by the servants as "the master's cat," because of his devotion to my father. He was always with him, and used to follow him about the garden like a dog, and sit with him while he wrote.

—MAMIE DICKENS, daughter of Charles Dickens,
My Father as I Recall Him

I wish I could write as mysterious as a cat.

—EDGAR ALLAN POE

He had a habit of coming to my study in the morning, sitting quietly by my side or on the table for hours, watching the pen run over the paper, occasionally swinging his tail round for a blotter, and then going to sleep among the papers by the inkstand.

—CHARLES DUDLEY WARNER

A Poet's Cat, sedate and grave
As poet well could wish to have,
Was much addicted to inquire
For nooks to which she might retire,
And where, secure as mouse in chink,
She might repose, or sit and think.

—WILLIAM COWPER

Authors like cats because they are such quiet, lovable, wise creatures, and cats like authors for the same reasons.

—ROBERTSON DAVIES

Famous Felines

Personally, I don't believe felines are a fad. We're here to stay.

—MORRIS THE CAT, 9Lives spokescat

I really am a cat transformed into a woman.

—BRIGITTE BARDOT

The sound of a can opener is the only thing that makes me feel truly alive.

—SALEM THE CAT, *Sabrina the Teenage Witch*

I am Catwoman... Hear me roar.

—CATWOMAN (Michelle Pfeiffer), *Batman Returns*

When I get upset, Mr. Bigglesworth gets upset. And when Mr. Bigglesworth gets upset, people DIE.

—DR. EVIL (Mike Myers), on his cat Mr. Bigglesworth, *Austin Powers: International Man of Mystery*

Cats are poetry in motion. Dogs are gibberish in neutral.

—GARFIELD THE CAT, created by Jim Davis

"I know some new tricks," said the Cat in the Hat. "A lot of good tricks. I will show them to you. Your mother will not mind at all if I do."

—THE CAT IN THE HAT, created by Dr. Seuss

"Wow! Do you know what that is? That's Schrödinger's cat!"

"No it's not, not anymore; it's my cat," I said, unreasonably offended.

—URSULA K. LE GUIN, "Schrödinger's Cat"

"Ack! Phht!"

—BILL THE CAT, created by Berkeley Breathed

"I didn't know that Cheshire cats always grinned; in fact, I didn't know that cats could grin."

"They all can," said the Duchess, "and most of 'em do."

"I don't know of any that do," Alice said…

"You don't know much," said the Duchess, "and that's a fact."

—LEWIS CARROLL, *Alice's Adventures in Wonderland*

The Superiority of Cats

The way to get on with a cat is to treat it as an equal—or even better, as the superior it knows itself to be.

—ELIZABETH PETERS

But thou, from cares like this exempt,
Our follies dost serenely scan,
Professing thus their just contempt
For Man.

—ALFRED DENIS GODLEY, "The College Cat"

The real objection to the great majority of cats is their insufferable air of superiority.

>   —P. G. WODEHOUSE, "The Story of Webster"

Calm, in consciousness of merit,
Sits the Cat upon the roof.

>   —J. V. VON SCHEFFEL,
>   "Songs of the Tomcat Hiddigeigei"

You walk as king scorning his subjects
You flirt with me as a concubine in robes of silk.

>   —AMY LOWELL, "To Winky"

I can't see what it is that makes a cat believe that he is so everlastingly superior to all the men that have ever lived, but there's no denying the fact that such is his belief, and he acts accordingly.

>   —W. L. ALDEN, "The Yellow Terror"

Even if you know you're superior to everyone in the room, don't gloat.

—GLENN DROMGOOLE, *What Cats Teach Us*

A cat can be trusted to purr when she is pleased, which is more than can be said for human beings.

—WILLIAM RALPH INGE, *Rustic Moralist*

Gentlemen, I used to have a cat here, by the name of Tom Quartz... He was a large gray one of the Tom specie, an' he had more hard, natchral sense than any man in this camp—'n' a power of dignity—he wouldn't let the Guv'nor of Californy be familiar with him.

—MARK TWAIN, "Tom Quartz"

I have studied many philosophers and many cats. The wisdom of cats is infinitely superior.

—HIPPOLYTE TAINE, French historian

I am the Cat of Cats. I am
The everlasting cat!
Cunning and old and sleek as jam,
The everlasting cat!

—WILLIAM BRIGHTY RANDS,
"Kitty: What She Thinks of Herself"

Your rat tail is all the fashion now. I prefer a bushy plume, carried straight up. You are Siamese and your ancestors lived in trees. Mine lived in palaces. It has been suggested to me that I am a bit of a snob. How true! I prefer to be.

—RAYMOND CHANDLER, letter from Chandler's cat
Taki to Mike Gibbud, Esq., "A Siamese Cat of
Imperfect Bloodline," Christmas 1948

A cat's got her own opinion of human beings. She doesn't say much, but you can tell enough to make you anxious not to hear the whole of it.

—JEROME K. JEROME